Are You a BULLY?

Addy Ferguson

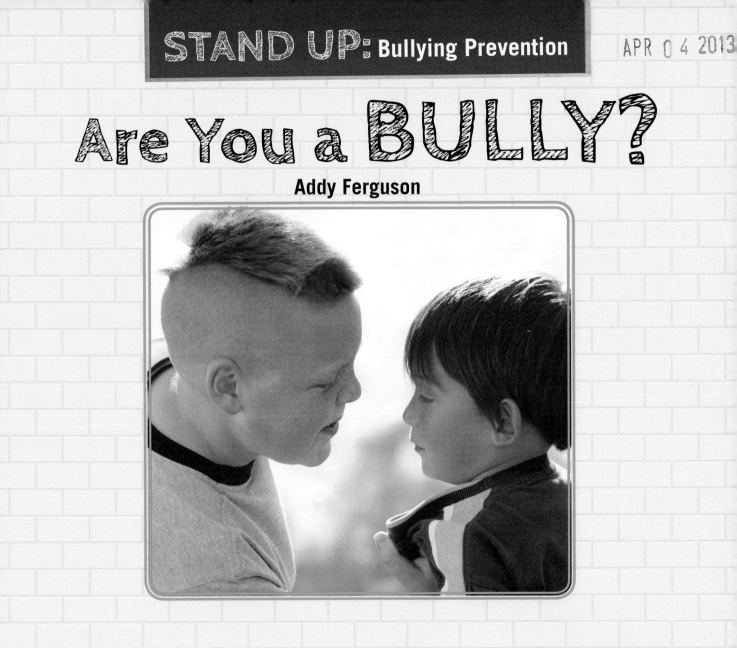

PowerKiDS
press.

New York

Published in 2013 by The Rosen Publishing Group, Inc.
29 East 21st Street, New York, NY 10010

First Edition

Editor: Jennifer Way
Book Design: Erica Clendening and Colleen Bialecki

Photo Credits: Cover Design Pics/Don Hammon/Getty Images; p. 5 Stuart Fox/Getty Images; p. 6 Laurence Mouton/PhotoAlto/Getty Images; p. 7 © iStockphoto.com/Ana Abejon; p. 8 Blend Images/REB Images/The Agency Collection/Getty Images; p. 9 © iStockphoto.com/Kali9; p. 10 © iStockphoto.com/Juan Monino; p. 11 Howard Grey/Stone/Getty Images; p. 12 © iStockphoto.com/Slobodan Vasic; p. 13 Winky Lewis/Aurora/Getty Images; p. 15 Katrina Wittkamp/Digital Vision/Getty Images; p. 16 John Howard/Lifesize/Getty Images; p. 17 © iStockphoto.com/Sturti; p. 18 Lynn Koenig/Flickr/Getty Images; p. 19 Vstock LLC/Getty Images; p. 20 Christopher Futcher/The Agency Collection/Getty Images; p. 21 Monkey Business Images/The Agency Collection/Getty Images; p. 22 © iStockphoto.com/Adam Kazmierski.

Library of Congress Cataloging-in-Publication Data

Ferguson, Addy.
 Are you a bully? / by Addy Ferguson. — 1st ed.
    p. cm. — (Stand up: bullying prevention)
 Includes index.
 ISBN 978-1-4488-9666-0 (library binding) — ISBN 978-1-4488-9790-2 (pbk.) —
 ISBN 978-1-4488-9791-9 (6-pack)
 1. Bullying—Juvenile literature. 2. Aggressiveness in children—Juvenile literature. I. Title.
 BF637.B85F467 2013
 302.34'3—dc23

2012022940

Manufactured in the United States of America

CPSIA Compliance Information: Batch #W13PK4: For Further Information contact Rosen Publishing, New York, New York at 1-800-237-9932

Contents

What Is Bullying?

Kids sometimes tease or pick on each other. This is not nice **behavior**, but it generally stops when the other person says, "Stop it." However, when someone continues to **taunt** another person, this is bullying. Bullies do not stop their taunting when the other person asks them to. In fact, the bullying sometimes gets worse.

Bullies can change, though. This book will give some ways for bullies to see what they are doing and understand why they are doing it. It will also give tips for how to stop and how to make things right with the people they have hurt.

If you have gotten into trouble for bullying other kids, it is time to change your behavior.

Kinds of Bullying

You may be surprised to learn that there are different kinds of bullies. Some bullies use words to hurt or scare their **victim**. These bullies are **verbal** bullies. Other bullies push things even further and **physically** hurt their victims. These might be the behaviors you think of as bullying, but there are other ways bullies hurt others.

Boys are more likely to use physical bullying than other types of bullying.

Spreading rumors, or mean and untrue stories, about another person is an example of something that a relational bully might do.

Relational bullies hurt others by keeping them from being friends with others. They **exclude** their victims and may try to get others to go along with them. Bullies can also use e-mail, texts, and social networks to attack people.

Are You a Bully?

If classmates have ever called you a bully, stop and think about why that is. Are you bigger, stronger, or more popular than other kids? Do you use these features to make others feel bad? Do you find yourself acting with force without thinking about it? Do you find yourself thinking that your classmate deserves what you are doing to him?

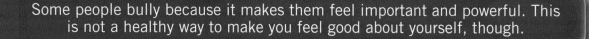

Some people bully because it makes them feel important and powerful. This is not a healthy way to make you feel good about yourself, though.

Kids may take part in group bullying someone because they feel like they have to do it to be part of the group. This feeling is called peer pressure.

Bullies sometimes do not know they are bullying. They are just used to treating other people a certain way. It does not seem wrong to them, it is just the way they have always been. Does this sound like you?

Behind the Bully

There are many reasons people are bullies. Sometimes a person bullies other people to feel better about herself. Sometimes bullies hurt others because they are angry about things in their own lives. Other times bullies treat people badly because they feel powerful when they can scare or hurt someone. Bullies may not like other people or feel very connected to others.

Even bullies who are popular and get good grades may feel angry or insecure about something deep inside of themselves.

Some bullies might have family problems, such as parents who argue a lot. These bullies may see yelling and fighting as the way to deal with problems.

Whatever the reason, if you or one of your classmates is a bully, it is important to know that people can learn to change their ways. It is not easy but it is worth it!

The Effects of Bullying

If you are a bully, you know how the bullying makes you feel. Stop and think about how it makes your victim feel. Then try to think about being the victim yourself. You would want the bullying to stop.

Kids who are bullied might find it hard to pay attention in class. Because of this, their grades might start to fall.

It is common for bullied kids to feel lonely and sad. This is because bullying hurts their self-esteem.

The effects of bullying can be serious and long lasting. Bullied kids may feel lonely or scared. Victims often **withdraw** from activities and friendships. They might start doing poorly in school or try to avoid going to school. They have low **self-esteem** and may have a hard time feeling good about themselves even after the bullying stops.

Talk to an Adult

Do you think that you might be a bully? Do you want to change your ways? What should you do?

Your first step should be to talk to a trusted adult, such as a parent or teacher. Tell this person what you are thinking or feeling. Don't be embarrassed. Don't be worried about getting in trouble. If you make it clear that you are trying to change, lots of people will want to help you. The person you talk to can help you make a plan for how to change your bullying behaviors.

When you are ready to change your behavior, you might talk to a teacher or guidance counselor. You can talk to her about why you bully.

Make It Right with Them

This next step is a hard one. You need to recognize what you did was wrong and make it right. You need to **apologize** to the people you have bullied.

Try writing out an apology. You might use it to practice what to say to your victim or send it to him. The most important part of an apology is to be honest about being sorry.

Teachers and principals must work together with students to create a school where everyone knows that bullying will not be tolerated.

Bullying hurts people, and your victim might not be willing to accept your apology. He may be angry with you or scared of you and mistrust you. Trust is something that must be earned over time. Remember also that actions speak louder than words. After you apologize, you must show your classmates that you have changed. Over time, people will begin to stop seeing you as a bully.

17

Make It Right with Yourself

If you have decided to stop bullying, you should feel proud that you are working to improve your behavior. Changing old habits or ways of thinking is hard work. Do not get **frustrated** or give up, though!

Writing down things you like about yourself will keep you focused on the changes you are making in your behavior.

Taking part in a charity event, such as a food drive, is a way to help other people. Helping other people is a positive way to improve your self-esteem.

Do not get down on yourself over the way you treated people in the past. Remember that you are doing the right thing now. If you were bullying because you felt bad about yourself, then one way to change is to work on your self-esteem. Write down the good qualities you have. Think of positive ways to deal with anger and frustration.

A Bully-Free School

Schools that work to create a bully-free zone understand that students learn better in a place where they feel safe. These schools have set up programs to help students and teachers work together to stop bullying.

Joining an antibullying group at school is a way you can be part of the school community that is working to stop bullying.

Schools that have big bullying problems are not healthy communities. If there is not an antibullying group at your school, you could suggest that one be started.

If you have been a bully in the past, getting involved in programs to stop bullying can be a great step to take. You will feel better about yourself and other students will learn to trust you again. If your school does not have an antibullying program, you can ask a teacher or parent to help you start one!

Everybody Deserves Respect

Sometimes bullies may try to place blame for their bullying on their victims. They may say they bully because of the way the victim acts or looks. No matter how different someone might be, nobody deserves to be bullied.

Everyone deserves **respect**. You do not have to like everyone, but it is up to you not to hurt others with your words or actions. This is an important change that you can make right now!

You are in control of your behavior. You can change it to stop bullying others.

Glossary

apologize (uh-PAH-leh-jyz) To tell someone you are sorry.

behavior (bee-HAY-vyur) Ways to act.

exclude (eks-KLOOD) To keep someone out or shut out.

frustrated (FRUS-trayt-ed) Upset.

physically (FIH-zih-kul-ee) Done with the body.

relational (rih-LAY-shnul) Having to do with the ties between people.

respect (rih-SPEKT) Thinking highly of someone or something.

self-esteem (self-uh-STEEM) Happiness with oneself.

taunt (TONT) To make fun of someone else or hurt his or her feelings.

verbal (VER-bul) Using words.

victim (VIK-tim) A person or an animal that is harmed or killed.

withdraw (with-DRAW) To pull away from someone or something.

Index

B
behavior(s), 4, 6, 14, 18

C
classmate(s), 8, 11, 17

F
force, 8
friends, 7
friendships, 13

K
kids, 4, 8, 13
kinds, 6

L
lives, 10

P
parent, 14, 21
people, 4, 7, 9–11, 14, 16–17, 19
plan, 14

S
self-esteem, 13, 19
social networks, 7

T
taunting, 4
texts, 7
trust, 17

V
victim(s), 6–7, 12–13, 17, 22

Websites

Due to the changing nature of Internet links, PowerKids Press has developed an online list of websites related to the subject of this book. This site is updated regularly. Please use this link to access the list:
www.powerkidslinks.com/subp/bully/